JANE PACKER'S
GUIDE TO FLOWER ARRANGING

Photography by Paul Massey
Prop styling by Jo Barnes

JANE PACKER'S
GUIDE TO FLOWER ARRANGING

Easy techniques for fabulous flower arranging

RYLAND
PETERS
& SMALL
LONDON NEW YORK

Senior designer Megan Smith
Commissioning editor Annabel Morgan
Location research Jess Walton
Production Patricia Harrington
Art director Leslie Harrington
Publishing director Alison Starling

Prop styling Jo Barnes

First published in the
United States in 2008 by
Ryland Peters & Small
519 Broadway, 5th Floor
New York, NY 10012
www.rylandpeters.com

10 9 8 7 6 5 4 3 2 1

Text © Jane Packer 2008
Design and photographs
© Ryland Peters & Small 2008

ISBN: 978-1-84597-738-2

Library of Congress Cataloging-in-
Publication Data

Packer, Jane, 1959-
  Jane Packer's guide to flower arranging :
tips & techniques for beautiful flowers with
more than 25 step-by-step projects / by Jane
Packer ; photography by Paul Massey ; prop
styling by Jo Barnes. -- 1st ed.
    p. cm.
  Includes index.
  ISBN 978-1-84597-738-2
  1. Flower arrangement. I. Title.
  SB449.P2257 2008
  745.92--dc22
                                2008022681

Printed and bound in China

Contents

INTRODUCTION

WHEN I FIRST OPENED MY SHOP BACK IN 1982, it was a small place in London's James Street. Although I believed passionately that flowers added so much to an interior and that fashions in flowers were influenced by wider fashion trends, it took me some time to convince others. With a lot of help from certain magazine editors, I began to see my name mentioned in features that I had supplied flowers for. Slowly, my reputation grew, and so did the understanding that, for many businesses and homes, flowers had become more than just a token gesture—they were now a fashion statement.

By this time, we were inundated with requests to train with us, and so the idea of the Jane Packer flower school was born. The London school opened in 1990. Nearly twenty years later, it is located in Marylebone village at 32–34 New Cavendish Street, and I am amazed at how many people from all over the world have crossed the threshold. We have opened several stores and schools internationally—in New York, as well as in Tokyo, Korea, and, most recently, Kuwait—something I never imagined possible. Thank goodness now floristry and gardening have become well-respected creative industries. I am extremely proud to know that we have trained so many people in the Jane Packer philosophy, and that so many successful businesses have been influenced by our work.

Over the years I have been asked countless times to define my own personal style. It's an impossible task in many ways, as my taste and inspiration is constantly evolving and changing, in tune with other trends and fashions. However, what is important is learning and mastering basic floristry techniques, as this will enable you to change and adapt your own style as you encounter exciting new influences. This is what we teach at the Jane Packer schools and the ground that I cover in this book.

I've tried to cram as much as I can into the book, starting off with simple tied posies and progressing to intricate wired bouquets and large-scale pedestals, with so much in between. So, whether you want easily achievable looks for vases, dramatic table centerpieces, or even bridal bouquets, it's all here. Enjoy the book, and good luck. Who knows: maybe I'll meet you at one of our schools some day—I hope so!

BUYING FLOWERS

When you're shopping for flowers, you want fresh blooms that will enjoy a long vase life. Look out for firm petals, leaves, and stems, and flowers with a good number of buds that haven't yet opened.

There are also some telltale signs that inform you when blooms are past their best. I always look at the foliage—wilted, soft, and yellowing leaves (or stems) are an indication that flowers are old and tired and may have been left out of water for some time. Inspect the leaves and stems, too, avoiding any that are crushed or damaged.

With roses, peonies, or other large-petaled flowers, study the petals. If their veins are prominent, the flowers are dehydrated and not worth your hard-earned cash. Examine the base of the stems. If they are black or discolored, they haven't been cut for a while and have probably been hanging around for some time.

If you are doing the flowers for a party or wedding and want them to be at their peak, bear in mind that you may need to buy them at different times. Lilies, for example, take time to open, as do amaryllis and hyacinths. Allow enough time for them to come into flower; otherwise, the flowers will be green and your arrangements will lack color.

AMARYLLIS
These arrive from the grower in tight bud and will open slowly. The stems should be strong, and bright green, and will be crisp when cut.

CARNATIONS
These should be bought while still quite tight. If the petals are soft or curling inward and the center stamens are showing, avoid them. With young flowers, you will be able to brush the firm petals open with your hand.

LILIES
A full-blown lily is obviously in the late stages of its life. But sometimes lily stems are refrigerated, and their tight buds conceal the fact that they are past their best. Look out for drooping or wilting leaves.

SUMMER FLOWERS
Stocks, dahlias, delphiniums, scabious, and alliums all have soft stems that deteriorate quickly in water, turning soft and slimy if the water is not changed regularly.

TULIPS
Fresh tulip stems will make an audible squeaking sound when they rub together.

CONDITIONING AND REVIVING

I once purchased a huge number of stock flowers only for them to die overnight—panic! Thank goodness we are close to London's Covent Garden Market, so we dashed to buy more flowers and saved the day. My fatal error was storing the flowers, still in their cellophane wrappers, in a damp basement, the result being floppy, wilting flowers. Whatever the flower, as soon as you purchase it remove the cellophane and release the flowers from any bindings, so air can circulate freely between the blooms. Many times I see bunches of roses stored wrapped in cellophane. The giveaway is usually one or two brown petals among the heads. Avoid them like the plague, because as you unwrap the bunch it's very likely that a flurry of petals and whole heads will fall to the floor.

CONDITIONING CUT FLOWERS

When you get flowers home, it is important to re-cut the stems before arranging them. Stems dry out very quickly, leaving a surface that will not absorb any more water. Cut the stems at an angle to enlarge the surface area and enable more water to be taken up. Next, remove any foliage from the lower part of the stem. This will help keep the water clean. Often you'll find a little sachet of flower food attached to your flowers. Use it—it works. Flower food will help keep a vase clean and bacteria-free, prolonging the life of your flowers, as well as helping buds and flowers to open.

CONDITIONING FOLIAGE

When I first started working with flowers at the age of fifteen, it was my job to prepare the foliage. I had to spend hours outside in the cold, hammering woody stems. Poor little me, with my frozen hands! Now, years later, we are told that a quick sharp cut at an angle is far better for woody stems, as it doesn't damage the capillaries that take up the water. I wonder if I could sue on the grounds of cruelty?!

REVIVING FLOPPY HEADS

Flowers can be tricky. Roses, tulips, gerberas, and hydrangeas can all be sensitive and hang their heads. However, there is a quick and easy way to revive them. Take several sheets of paper that are strong enough to support the flowers (newspaper is fine). Lay the stems flat on the paper and tightly roll it around the flowers so any drooping heads are held completely upright. Re-cut the stems at an angle and plunge them into deep water. Leave for several hours, then unwrap. Presto: revived flowers!

ESSENTIAL EQUIPMENT

When it comes to working with flowers, there are a few basic items that you will use over and over again, some of which are illustrated below. Apart from these items, I think the most important thing has to be a good pair of florists' scissors—sturdy little devils that grip onto the flower stem as you cut. Some people prefer to use pruners (or a gardening knife), and if you're creating enormous displays, you probably will need one to slice

FLORISTS' TAPE

Shown here is Oasis tape—a sturdy tape used to hold floral foam firmly in a container. Other types of florists' tape are available. The thinner tape is used for covering wires for bridal or funeral work. It comes in rolls and is available in white, green, and brown. There are several brands available, but I prefer gutta percha.

SPOOL WIRE

Fine wire is available on spools and is used to support and strengthen delicate flowers, such as lily of the valley, or single leaves that require support to maintain their form or hold them in place. The wires shown above are heavier, and mainly used for decorative work or holding moss in place on wreaths and other arrangements.

TWINE AND STRING

String or twine is used for binding flowers together in a hand-tied bouquet. It's also used to bind moss to a frame. I like to use Oasis Bindwire. It looks just like twine, but is in fact a paper-covered wire that holds flowers together effortlessly.

through tough branches. If you are planning to make a lot of wire arrangements, invest in some wire cutters to snip through chicken wire or heavy florists' wire without ruining your scissors. Floral foam is another essential—it's used for arrangements that need to last for any length of time, as it holds flowers in place and provides them with water at the same time. A sharp knife is useful for cutting up large blocks of foam.

FLORISTS' WIRE

Wiring strengthens and supports flowers. Fine wire begins at 32–34 gauge and is cut into 15cm lengths. The 56-gauge wire is more supportive, while 71-gauge wire is stronger again, and is the most commonly used. Stronger, thicker 90-gauge wire is used to support heavy items such as fruit, pine cones, or large flowers.

PEARL-HEADED PINS

These are perfect for finishing the ribbon-covered handles on bridal bouquets, or holding in place leaves that have been wrapped around a group of stems. They can be purchased in a variety of colors, so can even become a major part of the design.

PRUNERS

Pruners are so useful when it comes to tackling strong stems—you'll find them invaluable if you're cutting woody foliage or other tough stems. Always keep them clean and sharp.

FLOWERS TO GIVE

CLASSIC FLAT BOUQUET

This hand-tied arrangement is an updated version of the traditional "flat" bouquet. The flower stems are left long, so the flowers can either be displayed as they come, or may be re-arranged by the recipient. Flat bouquets are the ideal gift for friends who enjoy arranging flowers.

INGREDIENTS

9 x stems alliums

10 x stems salvia leucantha

3 x stems eucalyptus

8 x stems Cool Water roses, stripped of their lower leaves

3 x ornamental cabbage heads

2 x purple-tinged hydrangea heads

spool of twine

1   Begin by taking three stems of allium and grouping them together so the heads are staggered in height. Cut a length of twine and tie them together two-thirds of the way down the stems. This forms the backbone for the bouquet, so it's important to choose flowers with strong stems.

2   Add three stems each of salvia and eucalyptus to the bunch of alliums, placing the salvias on one side and the eucalyptus on the other. Make sure the foliage curves away from the center. Tie together, two-thirds of the way down the stems.

3   Place the roses and the remaining alliums on top of the hand-tied bunch, with five roses on one side of the bouquet and three on the other. With a flat bouquet, the idea is to display the flowers rather than arranging them, so the taller pieces should be at the back and the shorter, larger-headed pieces at the front. Take the ornamental cabbages and gently open out the leaves for a more rounded, flowerlike effect.

4   Now place the two ornamental cabbages on top of the other flowers, toward the center. Finally, add the hydrangea heads, placing them just below the cabbages. Now grasp the stems tightly toward the bottom and tie them all securely in place. Neatly trim the ends into a "wheatsheaf" shape (the ends should be about a third of the total length of the arrangement). The bouquet is now complete.

OPPOSITE Flat bouquets began to lose popularity when the hand-tied posy arrived on the scene in the 1980s. In the bad old days, I remember seeing dreadful flat bouquets containing all the odds and ends from the florists' shop. Fortunately, things have moved on since then, and this luscious arrangement reinvents the flat bouquet's old-fashioned image.

THIS PAGE I love these Majolica white spray roses, with their porcelain pink tint. Here they are tucked in and around large-headed, creamy-white Blizzard roses. Flawless white hydrangea blooms are positioned toward the base of the bouquet, and variegated weigelia foliage is entwined among the flowers. The overall effect is soft and gentle— the perfect pew end at a wedding, or presented wrapped in tissue to celebrate the birth of a baby.

THIS PAGE Casually wrapped in brown paper and tied with brown cord, the overall effect of this flat bouquet is spontaneous chic. It's amazing how the wrapping can influence the look. The flowers are blood-red Grand Prix roses, cordyline foliage, and artichokes tinged with burgundy.

THIS PAGE A classic flat bouquet of tactile pussy willow, peony tulips, and pink roses. The rich burgundy foliage is photinia and skimmia, and was chosen to add depth to the gentle pinks.

CLASSIC HAND-TIED BOUQUET

The hand-tied bouquet has enjoyed years of popularity in Europe, where florists automatically spiral the stems as the customer selects their blooms. They are now one of the most popular floral presentations. Hand-tied bouquets are perfect gifts as the flowers are already arranged and only need be transferred to a vase.

INGREDIENTS

3 x stems amaryllis
15 x stems Amnesia roses
10 x stems Black Knight tulips
spool of twine
paper to wrap bouquet

1 Take one large flower head as the central point of the bouquet and tie the twine to the stem of this flower at the binding point—about 8 inches (20 cm) below the head. Hold the flower in your left hand. With your right hand, cluster several heads around the first flower, one at a time, winding the twine around the stems and rotating the bouquet in a counter-clockwise direction as you do so. Build up a circle of flower heads around the central flower.

2 Begin to build up a second circle of flowers around the first. Slant the stems at a gentle angle to create a rounded shape across the top of the bouquet. Make sure you continue to bind the stems at the same point. For example, if you start with a binding point of 8 inches (20 cm) below the flower heads, you must continue binding at this point.

3 As you continue to add stems, rotating the bouquet counter-clockwise as you work, you will see the bouquet of flowers gradually taking on an even, domed shape across the top.

4 Continue to add material until the bouquet is the desired size or all the flowers have been used.

5 Wind the twine around the binding point several times, then tie in a knot.

6 Cut off the ends of the flower stems so they are even. Their length depends on the height of the bouquet—for example, if the binding point is 8 inches (20 cm), then you should leave an 8-inch (20-cm) length of stem beneath this point.

OPPOSITE I love hand-tied bouquets, from small sweet posies to glamorous armfuls of flowers like this one. They have become the most ordered floral gift, partly due to the fact that they are so easy for the recipient to take care of—no need to rearrange the flowers; just trim the bottom of the stems and pop them in a vase.

7 Gather together a length of tissue and wrap around the stems, making sure that the two ends of the tissue are the same length where they meet.

8 Tie the tissue in place at the binding point or "waist," making sure it covers the stems. Here, I used soft cream tissue to enhance the flowers and add to the overall size and impact of the bouquet.

ABOVE A hand-tied bouquet of dramatically colored, densely massed flowers: red hydrangeas, scarlet amaryllis, burgundy dahlias, cotinus leaves, and a red-tinged succulent. The succulent was removed from its pot, and the roots were washed and covered in plastic wrap. It was then taped to a discarded stem that acts as the stem of the plant, allowing me to bind it in place like any other ingredient.

OPPOSITE I love this selection of roses: the faded ice-cream shades lend the arrangement a beguiling, almost melancholy charm and work so well with the dull metal of the champagne bucket. Note that a higher binding point on the bouquet means the flowers will be massed together more closely.

ABOVE & OPPOSITE Amazing textures make for amazing bouquets. When combining flowers, it's important to choose a variety of blooms in different shapes and sizes, so that each ingredient is clearly distinguishable. This lush hand-tied bouquet contains delicate Majolica spray roses, creamy white hydrangeas, huge-headed and aptly named Blizzard roses, vibrant green poppy heads, and strands of white-painted bear grass. The grass stems were bent into a loop and tied in at one end of the grass.

GROUPED HAND-TIED BOUQUET

I love this unusual style of hand-tied bouquet—grouping flowers into small posies by variety, then binding them together in a bouquet. My philosophy is to use flowers in a natural way, taking inspiration from the way they grow, rather than using dozens of different flowers dotted throughout, like some mass-market bouquets.

INGREDIENTS

9 x stems cordyline leaves
6 x stems Soutine roses
5 x amaranthus trails
8 x stems pink arums
6 x stems dark red roses,
such as Grand Prix
5 x stems cotinus foliage
spool of twine

1   Form the cordyline leaves into loops by folding
them over on themselves and tying the point of the
leaf to the stem with twine.

2   Strip the thorns and lower leaves from the rose
and amaranthus stems. Now begin to bind together
the single varieties of flower.

3   Make up four bunches altogether, each bunch
made up of one single variety of flower and
surrounded by cordyline leaves.

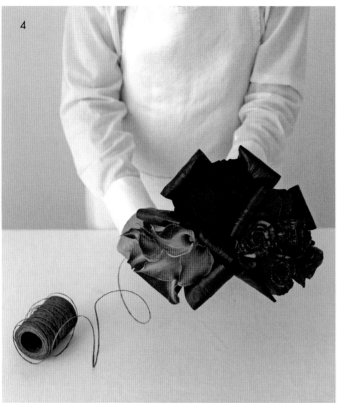

4 Tie together the bunched arums and the two varieties of rose, imagining that they occupy the 12 o'clock, 20 minutes after, and 20 minutes before positions on a clock face and leaving slight gaps between the three posies.

5 Add the amaranthus posy to the bouquet, then fill in the gaps between the other flowers with stems of dark burgundy cotinus.

6 Make sure you have turned the bouquet in the same direction while assembling it, so the stems form a neat spiral. Now trim the stems so they are all even, and place the bouquet in a vase.

THIS PAGE Use a tall vase to emphasize the drama of the amaranthus as it falls the length of the vase and tumbles onto the surface below. Amaranthus is also available in green, so you could recreate this look using green flowers and foliage.

THIS PAGE The same technique was used to create this soft pink bouquet. Individual bunches, consisting of roses, celosia, snowberries, and pink bouvardia, are wrapped in aspidistra leaves.

OPPOSITE Loops of thin ribbon are looped around Amnesia roses and cordyline leaves to enhance the color and add texture.

FLOWERS IN A LOW BASKET

Mention a basket arrangement, and it's easy to conjure up an image of those old-fashioned baskets with a huge hooped handle, filled with ghastly flowers that almost hurt your eyes with their clashing colors. It doesn't have to be like that! Choose a basket that you'd like to have in your home, and which will still see some use once the flowers are no more than a distant memory.

INGREDIENTS

6–7 stems variegated
cordyline leaves

3 x golden-yellow quince
or apples

9 x stems poppy heads

3 x ornamental cabbage heads

2 x artichokes

2 x green hydrangea heads

3 x stems gray brodea foliage

square of floral foam, cut to size

plastic liner or bin bag, cut to size

garden stakes for fruit

1   Start by preparing your materials. Trim the cordyline leaves at the base to make them shorter, slicing away the softer edges and leaving the central stem. Strip the foliage from the lower stems of the other ingredients and soak the floral foam in water until it is saturated.

2   Insert a stake into the base of each piece of fruit. Next line the basket with the plastic and insert the block of foam, allowing it to stand above the rim by an inch or two.

3   Start to insert the materials. The idea is for the arrangement to look natural and uncontrived. Starting from one side of the basket, mass the materials together and allow them to overhang the edges of the basket.

4   Gradually fill the basket, making sure it looks right from every angle. Around the edges of the basket, push the stems upward into the foam, so the flowers conceal the rim of the basket. The finished effect should have an abundant feel, with the flowers loosely grouped together so every angle provides a different aspect.

OPPOSITE I feel that this basket is suitable for so many different occasions and can be displayed in almost any situation—on a low table, or occupying the centre of a dining table. The basket has a late summer feel about it, due to the golden fruit and the faded green tones of the cabbages.

FLOWERS IN A TALL BASKET

I love this hatbox basket display. It feels very modern, with its tall cylindrical shape holding a grouping of single-variety flowers. The soft color of the basket demands gentle tones, whereas a darker basket could carry stronger colors. For several years we have featured on our website a bright pink hatbox filled with fabulous pink roses. The reaction has been phenomenal, so this "flowers in a basket" effect is obviously well loved.

INGREDIENTS

Approximately 20 x stems roses in a variety of lilac, pale pink, and darker pink shades
plastic liner
2 x blocks floral foam
tall basket with lid
spool of wire
floral adhesive or tack

1   Soak the floral foam in water until it is saturated. Line the basket with plastic and fill it with the blocks of wet floral foam, allowing the foam to sit slightly above the rim of the basket. Trim the plastic liner to fit.

2   Insert a 4-inch (10-cm) section of rose stem into the center of the foam so it can hold the lid of the basket slightly open. If necessary, use floral adhesive or tack to hold the stem in place. Tie the basket lid to the base using a length of wire.

3   Once the basket is ready, prepare the roses. Remove all the thorns and foliage from the lower part of the stems. Take a large-headed rose and cut the stem to a length of about 2 inches (5 cm). Cut the end of the stem on an angle, so you can push the flower into the foam easily. Insert the flower smoothly into the foam, and repeat the process with another rose.

4   Fill the basket with the roses. Use larger-headed roses toward the center of the basket, and smaller roses toward the edges. Instead of grouping the varieties together, mix the colors for an attractive effect. The space between the lid and base should be crammed with roses bursting to get out.

OPPOSITE The traditional basket arrangement had fallen out of favor when I designed this hatbox basket. It's modern and stylish, and the basket can be used again afterward. It's also the simplicity of the flower choice that makes it work so well. I've seen many copies of this arrangement since it first appeared on our website, so now I am laying claim to the design!

FLOWERS IN A BAG

I am always searching for new ways in which to present my flowers, and recently discovered this lovely linen bag with its faded floral print. The bag needs the support of the acrylic box, which also contains the flowers and the water. Here's how to tackle it!

INGREDIENTS

5 x stems dark pink spray roses

8 x stems anemones

10 x stems purple hyacinth

6 x stems senecio foliage

square of plastic/cellophane

spool of twine

rigid plastic container that
fits inside bag (to act as
a support and liner)

cloth canvas bag

1   Following the instructions on pages 23–24,
make a hand-tied posy to the width of the opening
of the linen bag. Tie with twine, then trim the stems
to a length where the heads of the flowers will rest
on the opening of the the bag.

2   Cut a piece of plastic or cellophane large
enough to cover all the stems. Stand the posy in the
center of the plastic, gather up the edges, and tie it
at the binding point of the bouquet. Then, using
a pitcher or watering can, pour water through the
centre of the bouquet so that it fills the plastic bag.

3   Place the posy in the square plastic container
and then sit this in the bag. The gray senecio foliage
works perfectly with the black and white print, and
I think this makes the gift look completely
"finished" in terms of feel and design.

OPPOSITE I am constantly amazed by flowers and just how breathtakingly beautiful they are. This new purple variety of hyacinth is no exception. Just take a second to marvel at the purple stems against the spring green of its leaves.

HEART-SHAPED ARRANGEMENT

Filled with a dazzling selection of flawless red roses, this heart-shaped arrangement is a hugely romantic gesture. The inspiration behind this gift was the fantasy of a glamorous showgirl having extravagant flowers lavished upon her by a besotted admirer who wanted to declare his undying love!

INGREDIENTS

Approximately 80 x stems roses in four different varieties and colors. I used Grand Prix, Black Baccara, Tiramisu spray roses, and a striped rose called Soutine

1 x heart-shaped floral foam base

1 Soak the floral foam base in water until it is saturated. Prepare a group of roses at a time by removing all foliage and thorns and cutting the stems to about 1½–2 inches (3–5 cm) long. Begin by inserting a smaller-headed variety at the sides.

2 Gradually add more roses, using the larger-headed, more open blooms toward the center. Mix up the varieties as you cover the base, but mass each variety in groups of three or more heads.

3 Continue to add the blooms, making sure that, as you work, you create a slight pillowlike rise in the center and a curved shape at the top.

4 Once you have finished and the floral foam base is entirely covered, make sure the heart is allowed to drain off any excess water before it's put on display. Leave it overnight, if possible, so it will not leak and damage any surfaces when finished.

OVERLEAF This slightly brownish-tinged spray rose with intriguing paler undersides on the petals is called Tiramisu.

THIS PAGE An extravagant arrangement of roses is the perfect declaration of love for many different occasions—Valentine's Day, an engagement or a wedding gift. This luscious rose heart, propped up on a dressing table, red lipstick at hand, makes me think of some glamorous 1950's diva who has received a gift from an adoring fan.

FLOWERS FOR THE HOME

DIFFERENT VASE SHAPES

Vases and containers of all colors, shapes, and sizes are the tools of the trade for passionate flower lovers. "Not another vase!" my son or daughter will exclaim in exasperation. I respond with a shrug of the shoulders, because vases are so important—they are the key to everything I do.

CHOOSING VASES

Vase shapes, textures, and colors are now led by trends from the worlds of fashion and interiors. We've spent a whole decade or more toying with clear glass vases, but now at last it seems that colored glass and ceramics are back with a vengeance, and a long list of young ceramists, as well as major stores, are riding on the crest of this fashionable new wave.

CUBE VASE

The cube vase has been enormously popular and important in flower arranging during the past ten years. It's a great little vase to present a bunch of short stems in a clean, modern way—think anemones, tulips, or peonies. All flowers can be used in a cube, but what's important is having enough blooms to fill it. If your flowers need a little help to stay upright, use a grid of tape across the top (this will work on larger vases, too). Use the grid just as traditional flower arrangers use chicken wire, and push stems through the holes. Just remember to put the water in first, as wet tape does not stick!

BUD VASE

Bud vases have a narrow neck that's designed to hold and showcase one perfect bloom. I love them. How often do you break a flower head off when arranging flowers, yet can't bring yourself to throw it away? This is where the bud vase comes into its own. Or perhaps you look into your garden on a chilly spring morning, as I sometimes do, and see a single beautiful camellia flower. By the time you return home, it has disappeared in the evening darkness. Cut it, display it in a bud vase, and revel in its singular beauty. I have been known to use test tubes, tea cups, and even milk bottles, as bud vases—experiment with different vessels and see how a single flower can bring them to life.

FLARED VASE

The flared vase is probably the most common vase available, yet it can be the most problematic in terms of shape. Use too few flowers, and you'll see your stems fall around the edge, leaving the center empty. Start by placing stems around the edge working in one direction—clockwise, say. Continue in this manner, using larger blooms toward the center and smaller flowers or foliage around the edge. There's a traditional rule that's a good one—stems should be no longer than the height and a half of the container. You can go shorter, but not taller.

TALL VASES

Use a tall straight vase to showcase tall dramatic flowers. A straight vase will hold flowers upright, so reserve them for strong, straight stems such as lilies, agapanthus, delphinium, and gladioli.

PITCHERS

Pitchers immediately suggest a relaxed country look. But this does depend on the material and color. A tall slender glass pitcher can appear completely contemporary, demanding sympathetic surroundings.

OPPOSITE Any avid flower arranger needs to build up a personal collection of vases in different shapes, sizes, and textures. A good variety of shape and color is important. Vases needn't be expensive—they can vary from something picked up in a flea market or chain store to a valuable collectible.

SIMPLE CUBE VASE

When it comes to cube vases, there are many variations on the main theme: they are available in everything from clear glass to handmade ceramics. A cube should be the simplest vase of all to use. Just pop a mass of flowers into it, and you're home and dry. If you don't have many flowers, or the stems are long, try tying them together just below the flower heads to create a massed effect. This little trick of the trade works every time.

INGREDIENTS

16 x stems roses

1 roll of clear tape or spool
of florists' tape

small cube vase

1   Fill the vase half full of water. Using the tape, create a grid across the top of the vase, making sure the spacing is regular.

2   For this design, where the flowers' heads sit very squarely on the rim of the vase, the stems need to be perfectly level, so make sure they are all cut to exactly the same length.

OVERLEAF This orange glass cube vase screams absolute simplicity, but it works so well illuminating a dark corner. Line up three or four of these vases to act as centerpieces at a longer table. The effect is dramatic.

BUD VASES

THIS PAGE I marvel at this modern take on the bud vase (left). Does it remind you of anything? For me, it brings to mind a baby bird reaching up to be fed. As this is a dramatic piece, I've used a couple of stems that do not compete, but instead enhance the shape of the vase.

I find bud vases delightful—they're fun to play around and experiment with. The choice of flowers is obviously important, as is the choice of vase. Use a glass, metal, or plastic container, or even a pretty perfume bottle, to get the look right. Place a bud vase by your bedside to make you smile in the morning, or by the sink, so you can contemplate a single perfect bloom as you wash the dishes. Snip one flawless specimen from the garden, or use a broken-off head from a bunch you bought earlier. You aren't limited to one bud vase, either—increase impact by lining them up along a mantelpiece or choose vases of different heights and pop a single bloom in each one before grouping them together in the center of a circular table.

THIS PAGE A grouping of small bud vases brings color and life to a small side table. The two central vases are by Jonathan Adler— I am a great admirer of his work and stock his vases in my shop. I think they work as ornaments as well as when holding flowers. With their different shapes and sizes, these vases hold a variety of perfect single specimens and allow each one's individual beauty to be appreciated. On the left, a bright pink camellia opens to reveal a fringing of golden stamens. Next, multipetaled peony tulips, apricot pink in color and flecked with green, balance out the plump belly of the vase. In the tiny curvaceous vessel at the front, spring's green hellebores lift the spirits. And on the right a dimpled vase holds velvety purple-blue primulas and a zingy apple-green guelder rose.

SIMPLE FLARED VASES

THIS PAGE The flared vase is perhaps the most common vase shape, but it can be tricky to get to grips with. The rule to remember is that the wider the mouth of the vase, the more flowers are needed to fill it. Here I've used several heads of hydrangea to fill the vase. These would work well alone, but here I have also added height for a more dramatic effect. Long stems of pussy willow power up through the center of the hydrangeas, their soft buds tying in with the color of the vase and the other flowers. Then, if desired, insert a few larger flowers. I've used plump peony tulips, but peonies or amaryllis would work equally well.

THIS PAGE A neat dome of massed tulips are surrounded by a collar of almost black aralia foliage. This time, the flowers sit low, just above the rim of the vase, for a modern effect. Notice that all the leaves have been removed from the tulips. This looks much cleaner, and also means that bacteria will not develop so quickly.

GROUPED VASES OF DIFFERING HEIGHT

I love this look. It's so crisp and modern. Instead of using just one vase, divide your flowers into groups according to variety, height, or color, then arrange them in separate vases of different shape and height. It can make more of the flowers you have. Or, if you've been given a bouquet with an odd mix of flowers, this idea will make them work together much better.

1   Remove all the foliage from the gentian and hydrangea stems, so that they will fit easily into the narrow necks of the vases. Removing foliage will also help to keep decay at bay. Cut the stems at an angle to allow the flowers to take up plenty of water. Now fill both the vases half full with water.

2   Insert the gentians into the taller vase. Their long stems exaggerate its height and slenderness.

3   Now cut the stems of the hydrangeas to length. Their full, round heads should sit just on the rim of the shorter round vase, so no stem shows.

OPPOSITE Play around with the two vases until you arrange them in a pleasing position. I like to position the smaller vase just in front of and slightly overlapping the taller vase to create a slightly random effect.

4 Now push the hydrangea stems into the shorter vase. Always use the larger blooms in a lower position to balance out the scale of the vases.

ABOVE Two similar vases in different sizes hold flowers in shades of white. The amaryllis stems have been bound together with twine just below the flower heads. The anemones were tied into a small, loose, domed posy that allows the heads to rest gently on the rim of the lower vase.

OPPOSITE The lower, gourd-shaped vase holds three vibrant lilac chrysanthemum heads clustered together and with their stems cut short so they sit on the rim of the vase. The tall cylindrical vase holds sprays of purple phalaenopsis orchids that curve protectively over the smaller vase to make a visual connection.

VASES OF DIFFERING SIZE

Arranging just one or two types of flower in a selection of different-sized vases creates impact and additional decorative effect. Here, the sugar-pink glass tank vases are a perfect match for the frilly petals of the hydrangeas and the fragile ranunculus. Low, wide containers like these call for a compact display of short, massed flowers.

2

INGREDIENTS

20 x pink hydrangea heads

4 x small bunches pale pink ranunculuses

3 or 4 identical vases in different sizes

1   Arrange the three vases on a flat work surface and fill them about a third full with water. Now start to put the flowers into the vases. Take your first hydrangea and snip the stem to length (you will have to vary the length of the hydrangea stems depending on which vase you arrange them in). The heads of the flowers should just rest above the rim of the vase, with no stem showing.

2   Continue to cut the hydrangea stems and arrange the flowers in the two large vases. Cluster the flowers together for a generous, massed effect.

3   Work from one side of the vase over to the other, adding the hydrangeas one by one. Pause to check the composition as you go along, so you can make sure the general effect and the color distribution is pleasing.

4   Once the two larger vases are complete, start to arrange the ranunculus in the smallest vase. Cut the stems to length and closely pack the flowers in, working from one side of the vase to the other.

THIS PAGE The lush, densely petaled ranunculus heads are even more breathtaking close up.

OPPOSITE The delicate pink hues of the flowers and the fragile texture of their petals are thrown into relief against the dark paneling of this hallway. The effect is that of a still-life painting.

LARGE VASE

I remember my grandfather bringing bunches of multicolored dahlias back from his allotment garden. They were wrapped in damp newspaper and would be handed over to my grandmother. There were other flowers, too—sweet peas, clove-scented "pinks," and Sweet Williams (which are in fact from the same *Dianthus* family as pinks). All very English country garden, yet place neon dahlias in a funky modern vase and you change the mood completely.

3

INGREDIENTS

40-50 x stems dahlias
15 x stems oak foliage
spool of florists' tape
large flowerpot-shaped vase
cellophane (if necessary)

1   Fill the container half full with water.
If the flower stems are shorter than the
depth of the vase, crumple cellophane and
push it into the base of the vase to
support the stems. Use florists' tape to
make a grid across the top of the vase.
The holes must be big enough to hold the
stems, yet small enough to support them.

2   Remove all the foliage from the stems.
Now begin to insert stems of the oak
foliage around the rim of the container.

3   Continue adding stems with the heads
massed together for a generous effect.
I have tweaked the more flexible stems
so they hang over the rim of the vase and
the finished look is not too rigid.

4   Add the flowers in color groups, just as
they would grow in the garden. You will
find that using a grid to support the
blooms makes things much easier.

THIS PAGE Linger over the incredible color and lustrous texture of this tight dahlia bud. Unbelievably beautiful!

OPPOSITE The finished article. A mass of clashing modern colors juxtaposed with somber surroundings, yet it works so well.

TABLE ARRANGEMENT

There was a time when I banned carnations and chrysanthemums from my shop. Oh, the arrogance of youth! In those days, way back in the early 1980s, I hated the rigid, knobbly stems of chrysanthemums. Since then, I've learned that it's not the flowers, it's just how you use them.

INGREDIENTS
50 x stems Princess Irene tulips
40 x stems orange carnations
2 spheres of floral foam
floral adhesive or tack
2 candlestick-style vases

1   Soak the two spheres of floral foam in water until they are saturated. Use floral adhesive to anchor them to the vases. Remove all foliage from the flower stems and cut them all 2 inches (5 cm) long. Using only one type of flower, start to insert the flower heads into the foam, working from one side of the sphere to the other, as shown.

2   Turn the sphere around and insert another row of flowers so the two rows cross. Once you've divided the sphere into four quarters, you can fill them in with the remaining flowers.

3   Having finished the first sphere, start on the second one, using the other variety of flower and working in exactly the same way.

4   Continue to insert flower heads until you have completely covered the second foam sphere. You need flowers with round, solid heads to create this sort of effect. Gerberas, dahlias, and roses would all make good alternatives to the carnations and tulips that I have used here. Remember to water the floral foam daily to keep the flowers in good condition for as long as possible.

OVERLEAF, LEFT These balls of orange flowers would make a bold statement on a reception desk, or as party centerpieces.

OVERLEAF, RIGHT The Princess Irene tulip is one of my favorites due to its vibrant coloring.

FLOWERS FOR
CELEBRATIONS

OVAL TABLE CENTERPIECE

This is a traditional table-center arrangement—the type used at dinner parties and weddings. I've tried to vamp it up a little by using interesting materials in shades of pink to give this old favorite a new lease on life.

INGREDIENTS

6 x stems pink lisianthus
2 x giant pink proteas
7 x smaller proteas
7 x ornamental cabbage heads, dyed pink
10 x stems gray brodea foliage
square of floral foam
spool of florists' tape

1   Tape the square of floral foam onto a shallow dish, making a cross shape so the foam is divided into four quarters. Remove the foliage from the flower stems and cut the ends at an angle so they enter the foam easily. Starting at the sides of the foam block, push the lisianthus stems into the center of each side at a slightly upward angle, so that they hang down and conceal the dish.

2   Continue to insert the flowers, using the taped dividers as a guide. Each side should have a similar distribution and arrangement of blooms. The dividers make the insertion of the stems much easier, as the stems do not collide inside the foam.

3   Now start on the top of the arrangement, first using more lisianthus. Always use smaller flower heads toward the edges of the arrangement and larger fuller flowers toward the center. Insert the two larger proteas near the middle, as they are the focal point. Next push in the ornamental cabbages, making sure they are evenly distributed.

4   Complete the display by filling any gaps with evenly distributed clusters of brodea foliage.

THIS PAGE & OPPOSITE
Notice how the lowest layer of
this arrangement sweeps down
and just rests on the surface of
the table. This is important, as you
want the base to be completely
concealed. If you have a long
narrow table, you may wish
to repeat the arrangement
at intervals along its length.

THIS PAGE & OPPOSITE This table centerpiece in shades of fresh acid green is made using exactly the same method as the centerpiece on the previous page, with a piece of floral foam as a base. If you are using floral foam in a vase, allow about 2 inches (5 cm) of the foam to project above the rim of the vase or container. This is to allow you to push stems into the sides at an upward angle, so the heads hang down slightly and conceal the rim of the container.

FLORAL GARLAND

There are several ways of making a garland. Those made using this method can either lie flat along a table, be wound around a pillar, or set around a doorframe. As the garland will be out of water, it's essential that it's made of sturdy flowers that won't wilt during the course of the day.

INGREDIENTS

6 x white hydrangea heads

6 x stems lime-green hellebores

12 x stems laurestinus

spool of twine or thick string

1   This quantity of flowers should make a garland of approximately 4 ft (1.2 m). Cut a piece of twine to the required length of the finished garland. Take the end of the spool of twine and use it to bind a cluster of hellebore leaves to the first piece of twine. At the base of the leaves, add a hydrangea head or a sprig of hellebore, making sure it covers the leaf stalks. Tie in place with the twine.

2   Continue to bind flowers and foliage to the main piece of twine. Position each new item just beneath the last addition to conceal any stalks.

3   As you add more flowers and foliage, make sure that you tightly bind each new piece to the last stem, so that the joined stems form a long extended backbone to the garland.

4   When you reach the end of the twine, reverse the flowers and add more material to conceal the end of the stems. Tie a knot and cut the twine. Lay the garland along the table. It's important to cover any surfaces that may be damaged by moisture from the garland. And, if you're hanging this around a doorway or a pillar, first make sure that the owners of the venue allow nails or screws!

THIS PAGE Garlands are a novel approach to table flowers—I think they look wonderful winding along a table and snaking in and out of flatware, glasses, and candles. This hydrangea garland has a blowsy retro charm that makes it perfect for a tea party. For a more contemporary effect, you could opt for a garland of trumpet-shaped white arums and glossy camellia foliage with frosted glass candle holders and tall slender glasses.

THIS PAGE & OPPOSITE

Another garland: this one has a pristine, wintry feel and is teamed with a matching wreath hanging on the wall behind. Both have been fashioned from silvery-green eucalyptus leaves adorned with glossy snowberries and their foliage, as well as apples that have been dipped into white paint. To continue the theme, I've used more apples as fun candle holders on the table.

THIS PAGE A lush garland of berried ivy snakes its way down a banister. It was tied in place with pieces of string hidden among the leaves. A matching wreath was made on a square frame. Ornate oversized tassels add another decorative element to the scheme.

OPPOSITE This simple Shaker-inspired garland of Douglas pine is draped along a mantelpiece. It is made from two separate garlands attached to each other at the center of the mantelpiece. A length of thin rope adorned with tassels covers the binding. To create the small hanging heart, I fashioned a heart shape from a length of thick florists' wire, then attached small pieces of pine using fine silver wire.

TRADITIONAL PEDESTAL ARRANGEMENT

A pedestal arrangement can be difficult. It's all about shape and balance. Too many flowers reaching in one direction, and the whole arrangement is likely to topple over. Not ideal in the middle of a wedding ceremony! They can also look old-fashioned, so a more adventurous container and pedestal will all make a difference.

INGREDIENTS

7 x stems dracaena leaves

8 x stems gladioli

3 x stems leucodendron

9 x stems cordyline leaves

8 x stems pepper berries

15 x stems large red roses

15 x stems red spray roses

10 x stems ilex berries

10 x stems red carnations

2 x artichokes

large blocks of floral foam
(enough to fill container)

spool of florists' tape

urn or similar container

1   Soak the floral foam in water until saturated. Fit it into the container and tape it in place. When you're working with a lot of flowers, you need a lot of foam—notice how it projects above the rim of the container by about 8 inches (20 cm). Begin by inserting the gladioli stems into the center of the foam. Now push the dracaena leaves into the foam on one side of the container and the leucodendron on the other. Position the stems at a downward angle, so they cover the top of the container.

2   Now add a cluster of spray rose stems both at the base of the arrangement and around the tall stems of gladioli on top.

3   Insert the branches of ilex berries so that they lean back slightly. Their weight will help to balance the container and that of the flowers.

4   Now fill in the triangular outline of the display using the large cordyline leaves. Keep the sides straight and not too rounded. As the arrangement is designed to stand in a corner or alcove or against a wall, there's no point in making it in the round. It should look like an all-around arrangement from the front or sides, but with a third missing at the back. Aim for a loose, slightly random effect rather than a very neat, symmetrical arrangement.

5   I like to keep the different flowers, such as these artichokes, grouped together. With a large display like this, you'll find it creates more impact. Place the artichokes at the center of the display, so they are the focal point. They should be the most prominent part of the arrangement, with the rest of the flowers gently curving back from this point.

6   Now fill in the gaps with the pepper berries, roses, and the carnations, until all the foam is hidden and the overall effect is pleasing. The finished arrangement will be heavy, so take care when moving it to its final position.

OPPOSITE It is so important to master the skill of building a good pedestal arrangement. Getting the balance and structure right is all-important for a dramatic and effective end result. In addition, the ingredients must be selected carefully. It's important to have a mix of flowers in different shapes and sizes, focusing on larger flowers toward the center.

MODERN PEDESTAL ARRANGEMENT

This is an updated version of the classic pedestal arrangement. It's a bold, structured piece that requires a large number of large-headed flowers. Here I've chosen a sunny, graphic yellow as the color scheme, but this type of arrangement would work just as well in softer, more muted shades.

INGREDIENTS
30 x ornamental cabbage heads
50 x stems sunflowers
40 x stems chrysanthemums
large block floral foam

1 Soak the floral foam block in a large sink (it will become very heavy, so take care when lifting it into place). Strip all the leaves from the stems, then cut them to 1½–2 inches (3–5 cm) long. Cut the ends at an angle so they enter the foam easily. Now, starting at the bottom, start to push the flower heads into the foam. Cluster the flowers together, so the foam does not show through.

2 Continue to add flowers, working upward and covering the front and sides. The back of the foam only needs to be covered in flowers if the piece will be seen in the round.

3 Gradually cover the front of the block with the flowers, then begin to cover the top and sides of the floral foam block. Mass the flowers together, but don't lose the square edges of the block.

4 When the block is completely covered with flowers and you are satisfied with the final effect, move it to its pedestal. The floral foam will hold a lot of water so, if possible, it is advisable to soak the block the day before making up the pedestal then let it drain overnight. This will minimize the chances of water slowly seeping from the arrangement, which might cause damage to a party venue.

THIS PAGE & OPPOSITE The block of flowers is positioned on a square pedestal of exactly the same dimensions. In a larger space, a higher pedestal could be used to spectacular effect. Blocks of flowers could also be made in three different sizes then grouped together for extra impact, but this would require a large budget, as so many flowers are used.

SEASONAL WREATH

Although wreaths are often associated with funerals, the wreath is in fact a symbol of eternity because of its circular shape, with no beginning or end. In the same way that we decorate our houses at Christmas, the spring wreath here is intended to celebrate the changing seasons.

INGREDIENTS

1 x pot muscari bulbs

1 x pot primula

10–12 x ivy leaves

1 x wire wreath frame

sphagnum moss for frame
and carpet moss to cover

spool of wire

florists' wire (71 and 90 gauge)

spool of florists' tape

glass candle holder

1   Attach one end of the spool wire to the wire frame and begin to bind on the sphagnum moss. Make sausage-shape rolls of moss, then lay them onto the frame until you have built up the desired wreath shape and covered the wire of the frame completely. As you work, bind the sphagnum moss in place using the spool wire.

2   Using lengths of 71g wire bent double into hairpin shapes, pin the carpet moss in place over the sphagnum moss to create a velvety-green base. Leave three small bare patches on the wreath— this is where you will attach the flowers.

3   Wash the soil from the muscari bulbs, leaving the roots intact. Position the bulbs on two of the bare patches on the wreath and push hairpin wires through the stems to hold the bulbs in place.

4 Using a heavier wire—I used 90 gauge—make two or three longer hairpin wires. Tape them securely to the back of the glass candle holder. Now carefully remove the primula from its plastic pot and gently ease the roots into the glass container.

5 Push the candle holder wires deep into the moss on the last bare patch, so that the glass holds fast to the wreath. Use additional hairpin wires to secure it, if necessary .

6 Finally use the large glossy ivy leaves to cover any gaps or uncovered patches of sphagnum moss. Overlap the ivy leaves so they look just as you would see them growing on the plant.

OPPOSITE Wreaths are something that I find immensely satisfying to make, whether it be a traditional evergreen Christmas example, or a seasonal variation on a theme, like this spring wreath. They are also very fitting as a token of regard or respect at a funeral. The wreath is a symbol of eternity that's suitable for almost all occasions.

THIS PAGE & OPPOSITE This flamboyant, dramatic wreath celebrates the onset of autumn. The molasses-colored chrysanthemum is called Tom Pearce and here it is clustered alongside the suedelike undersides of magnolia leaves and red-berried cotoneaster. The wreath was made on a floral foam base. I pushed in the flower and foliage stems before suspending it from a pair of antlers above this battered old leather chair. The small orange pumpkin was attached by pushing a plant stake into the flesh of the vegetable. I cut the other end of the stake into a sharp point, then pushed it into the foam base in a downward motion to hold it fast.

OPPOSITE Using large quantities of a single ingredient can create a bold impact, yet demands very little effort. This room has been decorated with glossy scarlet ilex (holly) berries. I placed small blocks of floral foam into the two small silver vases. The foam was cut to sit just below the rim of the container, then I snipped individual springs from an ilex berry branch and pushed them firmly down into the foam to hold them in place.

ABOVE The wreath was made on a floral foam base. If soaked in water and watered every other day, the foam will retain enough moisture to sustain the berries for weeks. Ilex berries are expensive, but the great thing about them is their long life span—kept hydrated and in a cool environment, they should remain plump and healthy for up to a month. The berries have a short season from November to the end of December.

CLASSIC HAND-TIED BRIDAL BOUQUET

There are three techniques when it comes to creating bridal bouquets: tying the flowers in a bouquet, wiring the flowers, or cutting the stems short and using a floral foam holder. In the last few years, the hand-tied bouquet has become the most popular option. It has several advantages: you can use delicate flowers that would not be suitable for any other technique simply because, with the stems still intact, you can pop it into water throughout the day to refresh it. Hand-tied bouquets take less time to construct than wired bouquets, which are a painstaking and time-consuming job, making them the more expensive option.

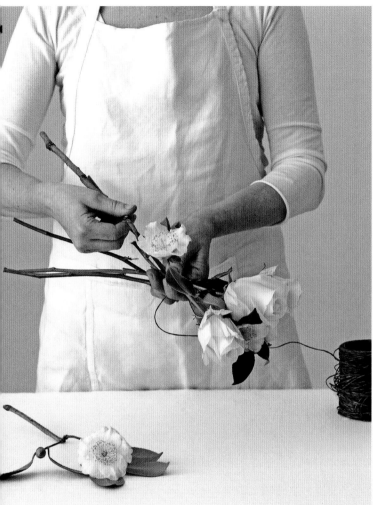

INGREDIENTS

8 x stems Blizzard roses

12 x stems white camellia with flowers, buds and leaves

spool of twine

3 ft (90 cm) ribbon

pearl-headed pins

1   This bouquet is made using the same technique as the hand-tied bouquet on pages 22–25. Begin by tying the twine to the central flower, in this case a large Blizzard rose. Turning the bouquet counter-clockwise, add more flowers to form a circle of flowers that surround the central flower.

2   Build up a second circle of flowers around the first, alternating camellias and roses. Keep the binding point the same. As you add more flowers, allow them to splay out to create a domed effect. Knot the twine and trim the stems so they are even.

3 To cover the stems, tie the ribbon at the binding point, just below the heads of the flowers. Leave approximately 12 inches (30 cm) of ribbon hanging down. Take the other end of the ribbon and begin to wrap it around the stems, pulling as tightly as you can. When you reach the bottom, start to wrap the ribbon upwards again, just as if you were applying a bandage. When you reach the binding point again, tie the ribbon into a knot, then a bow. Trim the ribbon ends to the required length.

4 Once the bow is in place, take a handful of the pearl-headed pins and begin to neatly push them into the bouquet handle at regular intervals, about an inch (2.5 cm) apart.

OPPOSITE To conceal the stems, I have used a faded peach ribbon that coordinates beautifully with the dress. The colors have a vintage feel: the fragile blossoms of the cream camellia, the vanilla hue of the rose, and the luster of the pearl-headed pins. Camellia foliage is strong and longlasting, so its robust leaves are good additions to any bouquet.

WIRING FLOWERS AND FOLIAGE

Wiring flowers calls for a lot of patience and painstaking care. The wiring replaces the flowers' bulky stems, allowing you to manipulate a flower or leaf into the desired shape and, most importantly, making the item much lighter. The thickness of the wire depends on the weight of the flower, but in general use as fine a wire as possible—it should be just strong enough to support the flower without the wire collapsing.

ROSES

If the rose is a variety that opens quickly, you may want to help it stay closed. Push a wire through the head of the rose and bend down both ends of the wire so they lie parallel with the stem. Wind one end of the wire around the stem and the other wire to support the head. Then trim and cover with florists' tape to finish.

LEAVES

To wire a leaf, turn it face down and insert a tiny "stitch" through the central vein about a third of the way down from the tip. Bend the ends of the wire down, forming a loop to support the leaf, and twist the ends round the stem. With this serrated leaf, I have pushed a wire into the main vein a third down from the tip.

BUDS

To support a tiny bud, use a fine 32-gauge silver wire. Push one end of the wire into the calyx (just below the petals or bud), then twist it down the stem. When you reach the bottom, add another, stronger wire then cover the wires with tape.

I have seen so many ugly bouquets that have been overwired and consquently are as solid as a rock and stiff as a board, with huge heavy handles made up of thick wire. The result is a bouquet with no movement and, to my mind, no charm. The bride ends up carrying this heavy weight around like a shield, rather than bearing a bridal bouquet that's a delicate, natural-looking assembly of flowers, buds, and foliage.

LARGER FLOWERS

A flower with a heavier head, such as a cymbidium orchid, needs a stronger supporting wire—a 71 gauge, say. Push a length of wire into the small amount of stem left on the base of the flower. To hold the flower in place, use fine 32-gauge silver wire inserted through the base of the flower head. Cover with florists' tape to finish.

LILY OF THE VALLEY

Something as delicate as this stem of lily of the valley needs an ultra-fine wire carefully wrapped around the stem and wound in and out of the individual bells. At the base of the stem, add what's known as a double-leg mount for extra support. Cover all the wiring with tape to finish.

CAMELLIAS

I've provided this camellia stem with a double-leg mount fashioned from heavier wire to provide extra support. Use a medium-weight 56-gauge or 71-gauge wire, bend it double and wind one end around the stem of the flower and the other wire. Trim the ends, and cover with florists' tape to finish.

CLASSIC WIRED BRIDAL BOUQUET

Putting together a wired bouquet is an incredibly skilled job, and great patience is required. Each flower, leaf, bud, and floret needs careful, painstaking wiring and taping. The plant stems are removed and replaced with wire, so that the flowers can be reconstructed into the shape required. This makes for an elaborate bouquet that does not bear much weight or a thick, clunky stem.

INGREDIENTS

3 x stems of hyacinths, divided into florets

15 x stems roses

3 x stems viburnum

2 x stems hellebore

3 ft (90 cm) ribbon

florists' wire (32-gauge spool wire, bundles of 32-gauge silver wire and heavier-weight 71- or 90-gauge wire)

spool of florists' tape

1   Start by carefully removing all the individual florets from the hyacinths. Now begin to thread them on wire for the bouquet's trails. Cut a length of fine 32-gauge spool wire, bend one end into a tiny knot and begin to thread on the hyacinth bells. Thread approximately 12–15 florets into strands, then double-leg mount the three strands together using 71-gauge wire. Cover the ends with tape.

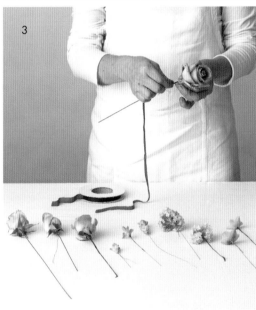

2   Wire the remaining flowers. Start with the strongest flowers and leave the most fragile until last. Take each rose and cut off the stem just beneath the head of the flower. Insert a 71-gauge wire into the remainder of the stem, then push a fine silver wire through the head. Twist the wires beneath the head around the small amount of stem. Try not to catch the sepals (the small leaves that surround the head).

3   Wire the hellebores and the viburnum by cutting the stems short and pushing fine wire into the remainder of the stem. Using fine 32-gauge wire, do the same to the remaining hyacinth florets.

4   Take a large rose as your focal flower. Tape a couple of hellebore flowers to the rose's wire stem, then add a cluster of hyacinths. Rotate and add a piece of viburnum. The first circle is complete.

5 Continue binding in flowers with the tape. Make sure you stretch the tape as you go—you'll find this will hold the wires together much more easily.

6 Add wired piece after wired piece until the flowers have all been used. Bend the wires to lean out slightly as you tape the flowers in. They should eventually reach a 45 degree angle, as shown.

OPPOSITE I've used a contrasting and unexpected vibrant pink ribbon to add just a nod to fashion. The bouquet is quite traditional in its soft gentle pastels, but the ribbon gives a colorful modern twist—a bit like adding pomegranate seeds to a green salad!

7 Trim the wires and thin out the handle. Make sure the ends of the wires are neat, with no sharp ends remaining. Add the hyacinth trails. Now start to wind tape around the handle, making sure it's perfectly smooth. This will help you attach the ribbon and prevent it from slipping.

8 To cover the stems, tie the ribbon just below the heads of the flowers. Leave approximately 10 inches (25 cm) of ribbon hanging down. Take the other end of the ribbon and begin to wrap it around the stems, pulling as tightly as you can. When you reach the bottom, wind the ribbon back up the handle, and when you reach the top, knot the two ends. Tie a bow and trim the ends of the ribbon.

THIS PAGE & OPPOSITE This wired bridal bouquet includes one of my favorite roses—the dreamy white Majolica. Here it's combined with mouthwatering hydrangeas with a hint of pink, orchids with raspberry pink throats and hypnotically scented lily of the valley.

WIRED CIRCLET

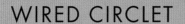

Circlets originally were worn as a symbol of eternity. At Greek weddings they are often made of orange blossom, as a symbol of fertility. At my own wedding, I wore a circlet of garden roses, burgundy amaranthus (love lies bleeding) and tiny clusters of burgundy grapes. The circlet was inspired by A Midsummer Night's Dream, *and I loved it!*

INGREDIENTS

7 x stems gardenias

1 x potted cyclamen

2 x stems white spray roses

spool of florists' tape

Florists' wire (32-gauge fine silver wire, and medium-weight 56-gauge or 71-gauge wire)

1   Firstly wire the gardenia and cyclamen leaves. Using 32-gauge fine silver wire, push a "stitch" through the central vein on the back of the leaf, approximately a third down from the tip. Shape the wire into a loop on the back of the leaf to support it. Push fine wire inside the cyclamen stems to strengthen them. Now wire the flowers. Use 56- or 71-gauge wire for the rose and gardenia heads. Cut the stems just below the flower heads and push the wire through the calyx, twisting it a couple of times at the base of the flower. Now add a double-leg mount (see page 119) to the base of the stem to extend it and offer extra support.

2   Cut the tape in half lengthways, so that it's really narrow. Cover all the bare wires with tape, stretching the tape and pulling it as thin as possible as you wind it around the wire.

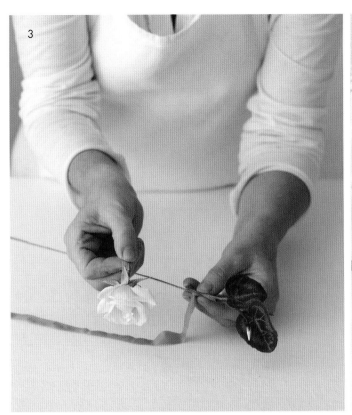

3   Cut a piece of wire for the base of the circlet. I'd use a sturdy 71-gauge wire or even wind two together to provide extra support. Measure the head of the wearer and to that length, add 1 inch (2.5 cm) extra at each end for the hooks that will hold the circlet together. Cut the wire to the correct length and tape it. Now begin to neatly tape on the other materials. Add leaves or flowers, alternating them on either side of the wire. This looks more natural, and means that when the wire is bent into shape there won't be gaps between the flowers.

4   Work your way along the wire, taping in the wired items and remembering to alternate flowers with foliage as you go.

5   Your taping should be clean and neat, with each leaf or flower "growing" away from the central vein, mimicking the way plants like ivy grow naturally.

6 Finally, bend over a neat hook at each end
of the wire to hold the two ends of the circlet
together. Now gently encourage the circlet into
a circular shape, and it's all ready to wear.

THIS PAGE & OPPOSITE
Gardenia flowers bruise
easily and require gentle
handling. Their fragrance
is hauntingly beautiful, and
a key ingredient of many
commercial perfumes. The
gardenia was the signature
flower of Billie Holiday, the
famous Blues singer.

FLOWER GIRL'S POMANDER

This pomander is gorgeous for little flower girls, but also looks stunning carried by a bride. It doesn't just have to be suspended from a ribbon—try substituting strands of plaited lily grass, lace, or even silver or gold chains complete with charms. With a little thought and imagination, you can make your bridal flowers a very personal statement.

INGREDIENTS

15 x stems Boyfriend roses
8 x stems Majolica spray roses
3 x small cineraria plants
3 ft (90 cm) ribbon
floral foam sphere
florists' wire (71 gauge)
spool of florists' tape

1   To make the ribbon handle for the pomander, fold the length of ribbon in half, then bend each end back by approximately 4 inches (10 cm). Take a strong piece of wire and bind it tightly around the end of the ribbon, as shown. Now use tape to bind the ribbon and wire together and keep them firmly in place. Soak the floral foam sphere in water until it is fully saturated, then leave it for a couple of hours to allow any excess water to drain away.

2   Take the floral foam sphere and push the wire through the center. Fold over any protruding ends and tuck them into the foam.

3   Start to add the flowers. Strip all the leaves from the stems, then cut the heads to a length of about 1½ inches (3 cm). Cut the ends of the stems at an angle so they can pierce the foam easily.

4   Group the different varieties of rose together in clusters of three or four, so the effect is loose and natural. The stems of the cineraria leaves can be quite soft, so if you have trouble pushing them into the foam you will need to wire the stems as shown on page 118, using a fine 32–34 gauge silver wire.

5   Gradually cover the foam sphere with the flowers and foliage until the surface is completely covered. Use the cineraria to fill any gaps. As with all wedding bouquets, this pomander should be transported in a box cushioned with masses of tissue paper, so that it arrives in perfect condition.

OPPOSITE So pretty and delicate, this pomander is perfect for little flower girls. Make sure the ball of flowers is firmly fixed to the ribbon, as little girls do tend to swing them around, and nobody wants pomanders bowling down the aisle!

ABOVE A tiny posy of lilac roses, silver-leafed cineraria, and purple pansies—a charming selection to decorate a cake or for a very young flower girl. These flowers have been tied together rather than wired, making it very simple to put together. I have repeatedly used lilac Boyfriend roses in the bridal flowers. This is to demonstrate how a theme or color scheme can be carried throughout, which works so well when done with conviction.

OPPOSITE A dainty flower girl gets ready for her big moment. Sweet-smelling freesias, delicate grape hyacinths, anemones, and full-blown dark purple hyacinths are all clustered together in a posy. The stems have been trimmed to a length that's easy for her to hold. A perfect "something blue" for the ceremony!

BEADED HEART CHAIRBACK

The cymbidium orchid is a perfect wedding flower, not only because of its flawless beauty and delicate perfume, but also due to its robust nature. The fleshy petals retain moisture well, making them perfect candidates for a long day out of water.

INGREDIENTS

3 x jasmine trails
2 x cymbidium orchids
small block of floral foam
plastic wrap
florists' wire (71 gauge)
spool of florists' tape
beaded cushioned heart with
hanging ribbon attached

1   Cut a cube of floral foam measuring
about 4 x 4 inches (10 x 10 cm). Soak the
floral foam in water until saturated. Let it
drain, then wrap it in plastic wrap. Cover
two 12-inch (30-cm) pieces of 71-gauge
wire with florists' tape. Push the pieces of
wire through the center of the foam at
right angles, forming a cross shape.

2   Take the jasmine trails and push them
into the foam above the wire.

3   Push the two orchid heads into the
foam, butting up to each other so they
cover the floral foam. Add more jasmine
foliage if necessary.

4   Bend the wires around the ribbon of
the heart, so the flowers are positioned
just beneath the ribbon and high on the
heart. Now loop the ribbon over the back
of the bride and groom's chairs.

THIS PAGE Just pause for a moment and drink in the beauty of this exquisite flower, the cymbidium orchid.

OPPOSITE This gorgeous chairback decoration is simple and easy to put together, yet looks so romantic and effective.

TRADITIONAL BOUTONNIERE

The classic white rose boutonnière has a beautiful simplicity. Teamed with a morning suit, there is no need for further embellishment. It's no longer a strict rule to wear white boutonnières at a wedding; now people choose a variety of flowers in many different colors. It's all about the style of the wedding and the groom's personality.

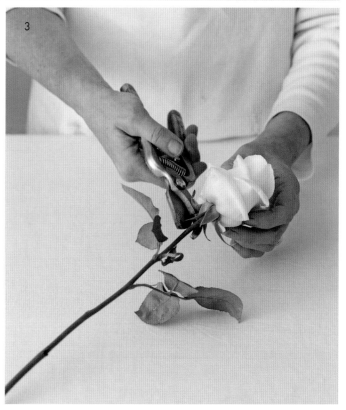

INGREDIENTS

1 x stem large white rose
3 x camellia leaves
spool of florists' tape
florists' wire (32-gauge fine
silver wire and 56- or 71-gauge
wire)

1   Prepare three leaves per boutonnière. Using the 32-gauge wire, make a small stitch on the back of the leaf, pushing it under the vein a third down from the tip of the leaf. Bend the wire down to the stem and wrap one end of the wire around the other end and the stem. Bend another wire in half and use that to extend the wire stem.

2   Cover the wires with florists' tape.

3   Take the rose and cut off the stem just beneath the head of the flower.

4   Insert a 56- or 71-gauge wire into the remainder of the stem. Now push a 56-gauge wire through the head of the rose, just above the calyx. Pull down both ends of the wire parallel to the stem.

5   Add the first camellia leaf to the rose, and bind all the wires together using florists' tape.

6   Add the remaining leaves to the rose, spacing them evenly. Cover any bare wires with florists' tape and trim the ends with pruners.

THIS PAGE & OPPOSITE
In the not-so-distant past, any gentleman with pretensions to style would sport a dainty boutonnière in his lapel. How sad that we have lost this tradition! Nowadays, it's mainly reserved for weddings, where it's usual for the bridegroom and other male members of the bridal party to wear boutonnières on their lapels.

LARGE CORSAGE

I love making corsages—they are quick to complete, yet provide a great deal of artistic satisfaction. Corsages are wired to make them lightweight, so they do not drag on delicate fabrics. Make sure the size of the corsage is appropriate for the wearer—being dwarfed by a huge corsage looks comical rather than elegant! Large corsages, like this one, can be pinned to a purse instead of a piece of clothing.

INGREDIENTS

1 x large central rose

2 x stems spray roses

1 x hydrangea head, divided into florets

1 x stem sedum, divided into florets

1 x sprig of rosemary

spool of florists' tape

florists' wire (32-gauge fine silver wire and 71-gauge wire)

1   Wire all the individual ingredients except the large rose with 32-gauge wire. Take the large rose and cut off the stem just beneath the head. Insert a 71-gauge wire into the remainder of the stem. Cover all the wires with florists' tape.

2   A corsage has three components— one large and one small triangle, and a focal flower (here it's the large rose). To make the triangles, start with one flower and build up a triangle shape. Bind the wires together with florists' tape.

3   Take the larger triangle and attach the large rose to it. The wired stems should all be pointing in the same direction.

4   Now position the smaller triangle below the rose head. Attach it to the main stem of the first triangle, bending the wire as necessary and using tape to secure.

OPPOSITE This sophisticated corsage in luscious shades of antique peach would be perfect for a bridesmaid or even for a bride to wear at a second wedding. Due to its generous size, it looks divine displayed on a vintage satin handbag.

THIS PAGE A far cry from the traditional wedding corsage, the candy-pink tones of this exotic orchid pop out from a bold tangerine jacket.

CHOOSING WEDDING FLOWERS

Your wedding day should be a time for you to indulge in the excitement and emotion of the big event and spend time with friends and family. In my experience, it's far better to leave the flowers to someone whose ability you trust—preferably a professional florist, but perhaps a friend who's an experienced and talented flower arranger and has had at least some experience of doing flowers at events before.

DESIGN

There are so many decisions to make surrounding a wedding. To my mind, the flowers are one of the most important elements. They will reinforce your chosen theme and, when used correctly, make a huge impact. Always opt for the florist that seems excited and inspired by your ideas or, if you are more open-minded, one that suggests new ideas to you.

BUDGET

A good florist will work with your budget, suggesting flowers that give you maximum effect for your outlay. I once decorated a venue with autumn leaves. The aisle was adorned with foliage; there were pedestal arrangements with branches of amber berries; and the tables were strewn with leaves and votives in amber holders. It looked magical, but didn't break the bank.

First impressions count. So don't be tempted to spread your budget thinly—one huge, extravagant display will be remembered, while six smaller arrangements that cost the same price will fade into the background without comment.

THEME

Clip cuttings of wedding flowers you like from magazines and work them around your color choice. Pinks suggest a soft feminine mood, red is a more vampish, sexy color, while whites can cover a spectrum of different moods, from purity to sophistication. Make sure you choose a color scheme that suits you, not just the venue carpet!

INDIVIDUALITY

Most brides that we meet at Jane Packer ask for "something different." This can be wonderful for the florist, as it presents the opportunity to be creative. But make sure the ideas do not date quickly—otherwise, your wedding photos will look embarrassing in only a couple of years. A wedding should reflect your tastes and emotions, so do not be bullied by well-meaning friends or relatives. On the other hand, this is your big day, so you don't want the flowers to look ordinary— they've got to be special!

SEASONALITY

The season in which your wedding takes place will have an impact on your choices. It will also impact on cost. Lily of the valley, for example, was originally available in spring alone. Now it's available throughout the year—at a high price! Out-of-season flowers can often be sourced if time is allowed, but this will have an impact on your budget. A good florist will know exactly what's available when, and suggest alternatives.

ATTENTION TO DETAIL

This is of the utmost importance when it comes to a wedding. Take swatches of fabric to your florist so that colors can be matched; look at any ribbons being used, or beads and trimmings. Flowers are a natural thing, and it's always possible for things to go wrong. If you are making your own bouquet, cover every angle by investing time in a trial run.

COLOR SWATCHES

One of the things I love most about flowers is the huge spectrum of colors that are on offer, from dramatic, moody reds and purples to luscious candied pastels to flawless, ethereal whites. When deciding on a color theme for a wedding or other celebration, it is helpful to know exactly which flowers are available in which

WHITES & CREAM
Roses, lilies, freesias, lilacs, hyacinths, carnations, hydrangeas, peonies, tulips, amaryllis, gladioli, alliums, agapanthus, stock, stephanotis, tuberose, gardenia, lily of the valley, delphiniums

YELLOW
Roses, lilies, freesias, chrysanthemums, sunflowers, ranunculus, carnations, eremurus, gladioli, honeysuckle, gerbera, iris, narcissus, forsythia, snapdragons, dahlias

ORANGE
Roses, lilies, carnations, gerbera, gladioli, tulips, marigolds, strelitzia, poppies, carthamus, celosia, banksia, dahlias, leucospermum

RED
Roses, carnations, lilies, anemones, amaranthus, celosia, amaryllis, tulips, ranunculus, peonies, heliconia, gerbera, gladioli, euphorbia, photinia, dahlias

colors. And whether arranging flowers at home or putting together the gifts in this book, I find that experimenting with color is one of the most creative (and enjoyable) parts of the process. When it comes to choosing flowers, I hope the color swatches below provide you with an inspiring starting point.

PINK

Roses, carnations, lilies, ranunculus, amaryllis, peonies, tulips, phlox, stock, proteas, hyacinths, hydrangeas, gerbera, gladioli, freesias, celosia, orchids

PURPLE & MAUVE

Roses, carnations, delphiniums, hyacinths, alliums, asters, agapanthus, orchids, hyacinths, iris, dahlias, anemones, tulips

BLUE

Delphiniums, hyacinths, hydrangeas, campanula, veronica, agapanthus, scabious, muscari, aconitum

GREEN

Roses, ranunculus, carnations, amaranthus, tulips, orchids, lilies, chrysanthemums, brassicas, poppy heads, iris, hydrangeas, hellebores, molucella

RESESOURCES

VASES AND CONTAINERS

ABC Carpet & Home
888 Broadway
New York, NY 10003
212 473 3000
Visit www.abchome.com for
details of a retail outlet near
you.
*Exotic collection of antique,
vintage and modern home
accessories, including artisan-
glazed tableware, handmade
bowls and handblown glass.*

Jonathan Adler
47 Greene Street
New York, NY 10013
212 941 8950
Visit www.jonathanadler.com
for details of their other
stores.
*Groovy retro-modern ceramics
that are guaranteed to make
a statement in any interior.*

Alabaster
597 Hayes Street
San Francisco, CA 94102
415 558 0482
www.alabastersf.com
*Unique collectibles and home
accessories that you won't
find anywhere else, including
pretty pressed glass pieces,
mercury glass vases, American
creamware, and English
transferware.*

Anthropologie
Rittenhouse Square
1801 Walnut Street
Philadelphia, PA 19103
215 568 2114
Visit www.anthropologie.com
to find a store near you.
*Vintage-inspired pieces, many
in glorious colours with quirky
details, making them look
more like antique pieces than
recent purchases. Also pretty
pitchers, cute tumblers, and
decorative bowls*

Brimfield Antique Show
Route 20
Brimfield, MA 01010
www.brimfieldshow.com
*This famous flea market runs
for a week in May, July, and
September.*

The Conran Shop
407 East 59th Street
New York, NY 10022
866 755 9079
www.conranusa.com
*Stylish tabletop accessories
including a large selection of
clear glass vases in all shapes
and sizes as well as
contemporary ceramics and
even funky plastic containers.*

Crate & Barrel
646 N. Michigan Avenue
Chicago, IL 60611
800 967 6696
Visit www.crateandbarrel.com
to find a store near you.
*Stylish vases at great prices,
ranging in style from the
simple to the fashionable to
the quirky.*

Finnish Gifts
www.finnishgifts.com
*Authorized retailer of the
Iittala Alvar Aalto free-
flowing glass vase, as
well as others.*

Fishs Eddy
889 Broadway
New York, NY 10003
212 420 9020
Call 1 877 347 4733 or visit
www.fishseddy.com for their
other two store locations.
*Pressed-glass pitchers in jewel
shades, as well as vintage-
style creamers and bud vases.*

Gump's
135 Post Street
San Francisco, CA 94108
800 882 8055
www.gumps.com
*Visit this luxury home
furnishings retailer for a
small but gorgeous selection
of vases, including some
striking floor vases.*

IKEA
1800 East McConnor Parkway
Schaumburg, IL 60173
Call 800 434 IKEA or visit
www.ikea.com to find a store
near you.
*Large selection of cheap-and-
cheerful vases, including cute
glass bud vases at a bargain
price. Many of their vases look
almost as good as their
designer counterparts.*

Macy's
Call 800 BUY-MACY or visit
www.macys.com to find a
store near you.
*Department store with a wide
selection of vases, both
traditional and modern in
style. Stockists of Kate
Spade's chic line of clear glass
vases, and funky Scandi-style
vases from Swedish company
Kosta Boda.*

MOMA Design Store
44 West 53rd Street
New York, NY 10022
800 447 6662
www.momastore.org
*Great selection of more
unusual vases, including some
intriguing and imaginative
bud vases that you won't see
anywhere else.*

Moss
150 Greene Street
New York, NY 10012
866 888 6677
www.mossonline.com
An exciting selection of striking vases in a variety of unexpected colors, materials, and shapes.

Neiman Marcus
Call 888 888 4757 or visit www.neimanmarcus.com to find a store near you.
These department stores carry a large selection of unusual vases from designers including Lladro, Baccarat, Armani Casa, and Lalique.

Pier One Imports
71 Fifth Avenue
New York, NY 10003
Call 212 206 1911 or visit www.pier1.com to find a store near you.
Seasonal selection of affordable, trend-led vases.

Pottery Barn
600 Broadway
New York, NY 10012
212 219 2420
Visit www.potterybarn.com to find a store near you.
Good-quality, good-value vases and containers whose eclectic good looks belie the low prices.

Rose Bowl Flea Market
100 Rose Bowl Drive
Pasadena, CA
323 560 7469
www.rgcshows.com
This famous fleamarket on the second Sunday of every month has everything from retro kitsch to antiques.

Ruby Beets Antiques
25 Washington Street
P.O. Box 1174
Sag Harbor, NY 11963
631 899 3275
www.rubybeets.com
Handblown, decorative 1960's Blenko glass and modern designs from Denmark's Holmegaard glass.

Target Stores
33 South Sixth Street
Minneapolis, MN 55402
888 304 4000
Visit www.target.com to find a store near you.
Inexpensive selection of vases. Particularly good for stocking up on clear glass vases in every shape and size imaginable.

William Yeoward
Visit www.williamyeoward crystal.com for a retail outlet near you.
Beautiful contemporary crystal from this talented designer.

FLOWER MARKETS

Van Haveren's Flowermarket
415 1st Street North
Minneapolis, MN 55401-4300
612 339 8242

Chelsea Wholesale Flower Market
75 Ninth Avenue
New York, NY 10011
212 620 7500

Greenmarket
Union Square Park
17th Street at Broadway
New York, NY 10003
212 477 3220
www.cenyc.org/greenmarket

Spring St Garden
1861 Spring St
New York, NY 10012
212 966 2015

California Farmers' Markets Association
830 Navaronne Way
Concord, CA 94518
800 806 3276
www.cafarmersmkts.com
A guide to local farmers' markets.

INDEX

Figures in italics indicate captions.

PICTURE CREDITS

Page **22** clear glass pitchers from Nicole Farhi Home (www.nicolefarhi.com); page **30**, from left to right, three ceramic vases by Rachel Dormor (www.racheldormor ceramics.com), and by Annette Bugansky (www.designnation.co.uk, +44 20 7320 2895); page **33** tall ceramic vase by Rachel Dormor (www.racheldormor ceramics.com); page **36** basket author's own; page **40** white textured vase by Annette Bugansky (www.designnation.co.uk, +44 20 7320 2895); page **41–43** woven basket by Voodoo Blue (www.voodooblue.co.uk, +44 20 8948 1818); page **44** plastic cube vase author's own; page **48** white porcelain vases by Bodo Sperlein (www.bodosperlein.com, +44 20 7633 9413); page **55** top shelf, from left to right, vases from Habitat (www.habitat.net), Jonathan Adler (www.jonathanadler.com), Habitat, Jonathan Adler, Jonathan Adler, Nicole Farhi Home (glass) (www.nicolefarhi.com), Habitat (ceramic), Nicole Farhi Home (glass). Worktop, from left to right, Nicole Farhi Home, LSA (clear fluted glass), Jonathan Adler (ceramic), Nicole Farhi home, Nicole Farhi home (glass), Habitat, LSA (white opaque glass) (www.lsa-international.com), stylist's own; page **56** orange cube vase author's own; Page **60** 'tall bird form' ceramic vase by Vivienne Foley (www.viviennefoley.com); Page **61** small white vase by Jonathan Adler (www.jonathanadler.com); pages **62–63** flared vases from LSA (www.lsa-international.com); pages **65–67** round 'Amoeba' blue vase from Scabetti (www.scabetti.co.uk) and tall vase stylist's own; page **66** blue vases stylist's own and Scabetti; page **68** white goblet vases from Designers Guild (www.designersguild.com); page **69** black curved vase by Jonathan Adler (www.jonathanadler.com); pages **71–73** pink glass tank vases author's own; pages **75–77** large orange ceramic vase author's own; pages **79–80** metallic lustre candlestick-shaped vases author's own; page **88** 'Tulip' dining chairs by Eero Saarinen from The Conran Shop (www.conranshop.co.uk, 020 7589 7401); pages **99–101** gold pedestal vase author's own; page **102** white ceramic vases from Zara Home (www.zarahome.com) and Habitat (www.habitat.net); page **117** dress from Orcini Vintage (+44 20 7937 2903); page **120** vase author's own; page **124** and **125** dress from Orcini Vintage (+44 20 7937 2903); page **127** suit by Oliver Spencer (www.oliverspencer.co.uk, +44 20 7491 2337); page **131** dress from Orcini Vintage (+44 20 7937 2903); page **132**, from left to right, vases from Jonathan Adler (www.jonathanadler.com), stylist's own, Nicole Farhi Home (www.nicolefarhi.com); page **146** suit by Oswald Boateng (www.oswaldboateng.co.uk, +44 20 7437 0620); page **148** white ceramic vases stylist's own.

Location on pages 2, 27, 35, 67, 68, 73, 77, 80, 96–97, 112–113 www.JJlocations.co.uk.

ACKNOWLEDGMENTS

This book has been an absolute joy to work on. The whole team gelled from day one and that makes a big difference when you are trying to get the last shot of the day and the sun is going down! I'd like to thank Alison Starling for commissioning this project. Thanks also to the talented Leslie Harrington and Megan Smith for their fantastic layouts, constant support and encouragement, and endless cups of tea! Thank you to Jo Barnes for her beautiful styling and for searching for the perfect vases. And of course thank you to the amazing Mr Paul Massey, for the most brilliant photographs.

Thank you to Annabel Morgan for tireless and patient chasing for bits of text, and to her daughter Antonia, our charming model, who shivered without complaint on a cold winter's day in her sheer flower girl's outfit.

Thanks to Adam Walkden and Trisha Dale for their work translating and organizing my untidy notes. And thank you, of course, to Susan, Emma, and Helen and the rest of the team at New Cavendish Street for their help every day; to Metz Van Cleef, our flower suppliers, for their support; and, last but not least, to my wonderful family, Gary, Rebby, and Lola, whom I love more than words can say.